ONLY ONE

SIMON AND SCHUSTER NEW YORK

NEW YORK

PHOTOGRAPHS BY JAN YOORS

TEXT BY CHARLES SAMUELS

PUBLISHED BY SIMON AND SCHUSTER, INC.
ROCKEFELLER CENTER, 630 FIFTH AVENUE
NEW YORK 20, N.Y.

First Printing

The authors and publisher are grateful for permission to reprint the following: Excerpt from the musical composition "Lonely House" by Kurt Weill and Langston Hughes, copyright 1946 by Kurt Weill and Langston Hughes, Chappell & Co., Inc., publisher and owner of allied rights; Letter from Delio on page 51 from "Bridge Without End," published by the House Council of East Harlem Projects House.

LIBRARY OF CONGRESS CATALOG CARD NUMBER: 64-25192
MANUFACTURED IN THE UNITED STATES OF AMERICA
PRINTED BY THE MURRAY PRINTING CO., FORGE VILLAGE, MASS.
BOUND BY AMERICAN BOOK–STRATFORD PRESS, NEW YORK
DESIGNED BY EVE METZ

CONTENTS

PREFACE

New York is not one city, but many; not one culture, but a multitude; not one city, but a hundred superimposed cities. We see it, daily, as a great, rich metropolis, dazzling to look at from a distance, seamy, often horrifying when looked at from street level.

But it is the *people* who make the city—not the expressways, the skyscrapers, the planning boards and the business firms. It is the people whose diversity is represented in this book, the people who prove that in this day of the robot there still exist everywhere surprise, excesses, passion and marvelous disorder.

From its beginnings, New York attracted the wild and adventurous ones, the bold and the daring in spirit. All things to all people: a springboard to great fortune for the few, a bazaar for the whole country, a final refuge for beggars and vagrants. But its most important function was as the port of entry, the gateway, for the greatest immigration in history. For those millions who came and the millions they left behind, it became the city of hopes and dreams and miracles. The multitudes who came brought more to the new country than they found. They transformed America and made New York the most international of all cities, the repository of cultures and traditions, many of which have long since become extinct in the countries where they originated. Between 1820 and 1930, thirty-eight million men, women and children came to the new country, the majority of them through New York. Millions of them stayed in the city.

These people brought everything they owned with them, not just the handful of silver in their pockets and the featherbeds they carried on their backs. They brought to the city the wealth of their own personalities, filled it with the music of many tongues and instruments. With them came their native cultures, foods and fashions, manners, ideas and dreams. Together, unknowingly, they transformed the city.

Most New Yorkers today are either immigrants or the children of people born abroad. The Government counts both as "foreign stock," and in 1960 its Census Bureau found in the city 859,000 Italians, 564,000 Russians and 389,000 Poles (most of them Jews), 324,000 Germans, 312,000 Irish, 220,000 Austrians, 175,000 British, 97,000 Hungarians. Also, 58,000 Czechoslovakians and more than 50,000 each from Greece, Rumania and Canada; more than 25,000 from Yugoslavia; about 10,000 each from the Netherlands, Denmark, Finland and Switzerland; more than 5,000 each from Portugal and Spain. There were 103,000 from Asian countries, 7,000 from Mexico.

Since World War I, of course, New York has become the home of a huge number of Negroes who left the South, hoping to find a better life in the great city. Today there are more than a million of them in Greater New York. There are more than a half million Puerto Ricans. They started coming in large numbers after World War II, drawn north, as others had been drawn west, by ambition, the hope of freedom, wanderlust—and the lure of the great city.

We know the worlds of the great immigration groups—St. Patrick is now as American as George Washington—but there are, within the city, a thousand, a hundred thousand, private worlds, where a life goes on that remains closed, private and unique, screened from us either by fear, by pride or by our own indifference. It is not just the world of Harlem with its grim poverty and its startling vitality and show. Nor the babel of religions, from Buddhism to African cults. Nor the unexpected glimpse of such unfamiliar people as American Indians and Gypsies. It is the excitement of many worlds within a *living* city that obeys no conventions, recognizes no stereotypes and accepts—indifferently—every sort of human behavior and tradition.

Everybody who loves New York also hates it at times. Was there ever anywhere a more pugnacious metropolis? The newcomer can sense the restlessness, the power, the tension: the city seems to seethe with inexhaustible fury as it reshapes itself daily, destroying the past, hurrying toward an unplanned future.

At times New York behaves as though it were trying to make amends for not having been so much as threatened by enemy attack in the past hundred and fifty years. It presents a constant scene of battle: the scarred and battered ruins, the beautiful old buildings devastated, gaping holes blasted into the shattered rock. . . . The planes roar overhead, the pneumatic drills rattle, the taxis trumpet at the ground level, the subway screams and rattles below. It is the noise of tomorrow, strident and harsh, impersonal and hectic, hiding from the casual observer the fact that men and women live their lives here, sheltering in the unique privacy of a city that by its size makes strangers of neighbors, and friends of strangers.

The reward of New York living is being both a participant and an observer of a great spectacle. For the New Yorker has two lives—his private life as an individual, and his life as a member of a community, always revealing itself in a never-ending series of comic, tragic, moving spectacles, from fires to festivals, from murders to weddings. The busy street is the New Yorker's theater and home.

This book is a collection of photographs designed not so much to show what life is like among the poor or the dispossessed—how they exist, we know all too well—but to record the immense and exotic beauty of a city that has no common culture, no dominant character. New York, more than any other great city, is a place where different groups, races and professions meet together, without abandoning their individuality and their pride in being *themselves.* Who can deny that life is hard for the Puerto Rican or the Negro? Who can deny that much must be done to improve their life? But the glory of New York is that they remain themselves, they are not forced to abandon their own habits and culture to assume another, homogenized, way of life, neither one thing nor another.

The images of this book are of *people,* in their pride, their misery, their happiness, their constant reaffirmation of individuality.

Here are the faces that are seldom seen.

FESTIVALS

IN THE DAYS when a tour of New York's Lower East Side was like a one-night trip around the world, visitors paid little attention to the annual Italian-American street festivals. They were just one more gay, interesting attraction in a neighborhood already flooded with the colors and the moods, native clothes and music of a dozen foreign lands.

The whole life of these newcomers seemed to be lived on these streets. Their markets were pushcarts, the grimy streets their village squares and *corsi*. There was also a Little Vienna, a Little Poland, a Little Budapest. Men played cards, read newspapers, smoked pipes in their cafés. Each was like a club. The Germans had their beer gardens, the Italians their wine stores. Music was played on zithers, violins, mandolins, street organs. People sang from fire escapes, barber shops, stores and backyards in half a dozen different languages. Italian couples, Bulgarian lovers danced in their native costumes on the streets. Not to display themselves: there just was no room to dance in their overcrowded tenement flats.

There was great evil in these slums, suffering, shocking exploitation—but there was also hope. And the newcomers sang and danced and made music because of the promise tomorrow held.

Tomorrow they might start a business, open a restaurant, buy a pushcart loaded down with food, clothing, fish, costume jewelry or fur coats, find the promise of the promised land.

Immigration virtually stopped during World War I. It was reduced to a trickle again by the 1924 Immigration Restriction Act. Gradually the color drained out of the Lower East Side and most other slums as the immigrants and their children became assimilated. With a handful of exceptions at certain times of the year, the slums became indistinguishable from one another and the people who had remained there became invisible. Only on nights of celebration are some streets bedecked again in gay colors, brightened with necklaces of electric lights, flags, bunting, with couples dancing on the streets to live music.

Of all the immigrants, those from Italy were among the most clannish. For one thing, they suffered from a double language handicap. Not only were they unable to understand a word of English, they were unable to understand one another unless they came from the same village or neighborhood. So the moment an Italian got here he tried to find his fellow villagers. He moved in with them, if there was room. If not, he made frantic efforts to get a room in their tenement, on the same floor, if possible. After they had been here a few years, those who had been neighbors in Italy as well as here and who attended the same Catholic church often decided to hold an annual fiesta—as similar as possible to the one they had reveled in as children.

One such group, Società di San Antonio, was organized in 1916. The members came from Nola, in Southern Italy, about twenty-two miles from Naples, and had settled on 108th Street, near the East River, and only a few blocks south of the site of the annual Our Lady of Mount Carmel celebration.

Today, a half-century later, the grandsons of the founders of the Società run the festival. The Società's thirty members are successful businessmen. Most of them have moved away from East Harlem to the Bronx, Brooklyn and the New Jersey suburbs. Each year about a dozen of them devote their summer vacations to making arrangements for the *festa,* which lasts five days and requires an investment of about nine thousand dollars.

There are the usual food stands along the street, which is lined with aging tenements and old stores on one side, a housing development on the other. There are games of luck and chance, as the carnival people call them, and for the children a merry-go-round, a Ferris wheel and even a small roller coaster. The profits from these attractions and contributions of one-dollar, five-dollar and ten-dollar bills pinned to a statue of St. Anthony of Padua in an open chapel have always paid expenses and three hundred to three thousand dollars in addition. All profits are donated to St. Ann, the neighborhood's Catholic church.

The most spectacular feature of this particular *festa* is the carrying up and down the street of an 82-foot tall tower decorated with images painted in many colors of St. Anthony, St. Paula, St. Rita and St. Theresa. Sitting on the platform is the band that plays music for the street dancing at the festival, a singer, four men who hold ropes to keep the great tower upright, three carpenters (there in case of emergency) and city officials. The tower, the platform and the men on it weigh five tons, it is said; 108 *paranze* are needed to carry it. They are chosen for their strength—and good character.

The annual celebration in Chinatown of the Chinese New Year has always drawn both tourists and the press. It begins with the exploding of firecrackers, forbidden elsewhere in the city, and the dance of paper lions (usually called dragons in the newspapers). With smoke issuing from their mouths and nostrils, the ferocious lions try to outdance and outmaneuver each other while drums beat and cymbals clash. The legend is that they frighten away evil spirits.

A week before this public ceremony, there takes place a more private, familial celebration, called *Sun Neen.* The God of the Kitchen (or Hearth God) is burned in the form of a paper effigy, after his lips have been "sealed" with honey—a bribe that is supposed to ensure his favor when he ascends to *Sheung Duy*, the Almighty, to report on the virtues and vices of each member of the family.

Despite the inroads of Americanization, tourism and urban renewal, Chinatown remains, under the gaudy surface, distinctly and profoundly Chinese. Even in the third generation, Chinese living here call themselves *Hua Chiao*, "sojourning Chinese"; and they support a host of activities, clubs, organizations and institutions, including a school, five Chinese motion picture theaters (in which the film is often in the Shanghai dialect, with Cantonese subtitles!), several magazines, musical and operatic clubs—and, of course, a complex of farms on Long Island that produce Chinese vegetables.

Festival of St. Anthony of Padua, East 108th Street, Manhattan.

DELICATESSEN
GROCERY

ABOVE: The flags of the tongs fly from the fire escapes of Chinatown. Chinese New Year.

AT LEFT: It is the custom in both the Chinese and the Italian festivals to pin offerings of money on the symbols of the procession—the Chinese fasten the bills to the flags, the Italians attach them to the shrine of the Madonna.

38
33
WING FAT CO.

新京
新京
Coffee Shop

Japanese Obon, Riverside Drive.

"In All of the Strange and Wondrous Ways Men Worship God"

THERE is no greater mark of the city's exuberant diversity than its churches. The great European cities are dominated by their cathedrals, symbols of the prevailing religion, overwhelming the other denominations and religions by their bulk, their age and their power. Not so in New York. St. Patrick's looms large in central Manhattan, but it is no more than one church among many, a giant in the hierarchy that descends, in size, to the store-front churches of a thousand sects.

More forms of worship can probably be found here than in any other city of the world. New York has hundreds of Catholic and Protestant churches, hundreds of Jewish synagogues; the names of the Eastern Orthodox churches alone fill more than half a column in Manhattan's classified telephone directory. These include Albanian Orthodox Church of St. Nicholas, All Saints Ukrainian Orthodox Church of New York, Greek St. Nicholas Church, Saint Barbara Greek Orthodox Church, Roumanian Orthodox Church of St. Dumitru, many Russian Orthodox churches. There are also Moravian, Mormon and Mennonite churches, a Buddhist temple, a Mohammedan mosque in Brooklyn—and many others, lesser known, including a Catholic church for American Indians, with a fresco of the Crucifixion in which Christ is an Indian. . . .

There are dozens of religious sects in Harlem alone, ranging from the conventional to the bizarre. The Black Muslims, now famous, have their places of worship there. So do the Yoruba, who have attempted to re-create the religious beliefs, the manners and the clothing of an Africa which they have never seen, and whose forms of worship they have taken not so much from ancient texts—as do most religions—but from the studies of scholars and anthropologists.

Their leader urges his followers to, "africanize everything! Our names, our hats, our clothes, homes, furnishings, businesses, holidays, arts, social functions, political parties, our manners and customs. . . . It is distinctly unnatural and degrading, even ridiculous, for persons of African descent to have to keep European customs and habits forced upon them during their enslavement."

Among the most famous of Negro religious groups is the United House of Prayer for All People of the Church on the Rock of the Apostolic Faith, better known to outsiders as "Daddy Grace's Church." The late Bishop Grace began his preaching in New Bedford, Massachusetts (where the first House of Prayer still stands), and said of himself, "As Noah was before the flood, so is Daddy Grace before the fire."

In New York and other cities the church has approximately 115 subchurches (known as "missions"), and it is made up of a series of suborganizations which combine religious and social activities—among them the Grace Soldiers, a special honor guard for the Bishop, groups known as Boy Scouts which work with children, choral groups and bands.

Bishop Grace has been succeeded in office by Bishop Walter McCollough, but the traditions and display of the church remain, as they have always been, flamboyant and powerfully moving—a blend of revivalism, ceremony, pageantry and music that is unique, a combination of antic frenzy, open confession and deep faith that makes the services extraordinary spectacles.

The Black Jews of Harlem call themselves "The Commandment Keepers," and have more than one thousand members. Their temple in Harlem is Bayis Hatefelo (Temple of the Living God). They claim that like the Falasha, the sixty thousand Black Jews in Ethiopia, they are descendants of King Solomon and the Queen of Sheba. They lead an austere life, observe the Jewish dietary laws and maintain close spiritual and sentimental relations with the Falasha.

Their leader is Rabbi Wentworth Arthur Matthew, a devout and pious man, who was ordained in 1931 (although for years the New York Board of Rabbis refused to accept him). Irving Black of New York's Reform Brotherhood Synagogue tried to get the Commandment Keepers recognized by all Jewry. "Any group of people," he argued, "who say they are Jewish and who follow the practices and traditions of Judaism are Jews." Another authority said, "Some of our Jews have not awakened to the fact that we are Jews by conviction and not by blood. There is no Jewish race and black as well as white Jews are equally members of the Jewish people." "We abhor the word Negro," said Rabbi Matthew. "I am an Afro-American and so are all of my children. Today we have sixteen million Negroes. Tomorrow we will have sixteen million Black Jews."

No miracle is more striking than the existence in New York of a flourishing Hasidic community. From time to time one sees the Hasidim in the streets, busy, preoccupied figures, standing out sharply from the crowd with their beards, their black kaftans and broad-brimmed hats, their faces unmistakably *foreign.* Once, their communities flourished in Poland, Russia and Hungary. Now, New York is their Jerusalem, the center of religion, a people and a set of traditions that have endured and survived every kind of persecution.

Hasidism was founded in 1734 by Rebbe Baal-Shem-Tov, who set out to make the Hebrew faith as accessible to the ignorant as it was to the Talmudic scholar. From this basically democratic and popular intention comes the Hasidic emphasis on joy and happiness—theirs is no somber religion, no tormented belief. At the same time, Hasidism is more than an adaptation or a simplification of orthodox Judaism. Its special prayers and ceremonies are derived from the Cabala, and it is from this foundation of cabalistic tradition that Hasidism derives its belief in reincarnation (*gilgul*), and in the transmigration of souls (*dybbuk*).

Hasidism is more than a religion—it is a world, firmly barred against outsiders, self-supporting, self-governing. It is divided into groups, each taking its name from its place of origin (Lubavitcher, Klausenburger, Lisker, Bobover, etc.), each led and governed by a Zaddik, commonly known as a "Miraculous Rabbi." Each rabbi passes his office on to his son or closest male relative, for among the Hasidim, the office of rabbi is hereditary. The rabbi reigns over an almost medieval court, called a *hoif,* in which he interprets the law, like a benevolent but firm monarch, gives decisions, has his own court musicians, purveyors, silversmiths. Their churches range from impressive synagogues to store-front *shtieblachs,* and the Zaddik, like an archbishop, controls innumerable churches. Unlike an archbishop, his churches and his flock may be scattered all over the world, for the individual Hasidic groups, wherever they are, remain faithful to their own Zaddik.

The Hasidim produce their own Kosher food; they manufacture religious goods, *tefillin, tallesim,* Hebrew books, silver ornaments. Some work in the diamond industry, some have been seen working at such Americanized jobs as "soda-jerking"; none has ever worked in the garment center.

Their ceremonies are unchanged, a curious blend of orthodox Judaism and Hasidic innovation. Before every Sabbath, they take the *mikva,* or ritual bath. At the closing of the Sabbath, they eat a communal meal together, ending in a dance of frenzied religious joy, as the men swing back and forth together in the sacred rhythms of Hasidic ecstasy. At weddings, the Hasidim have even been seen dancing on each others' shoulders, three tiers of dancers, circling swiftly around the synagogue like a human pyramid.

It is not an unusual sight to see bottles of liquor on a table in a Hasidic synagogue—for this is also a part of their worship and their joy. It is a religion in which food, drink, music, dance and prayer all are forms of devotion.

Hasidic Congregation Rabbi Hirschele Lisker.

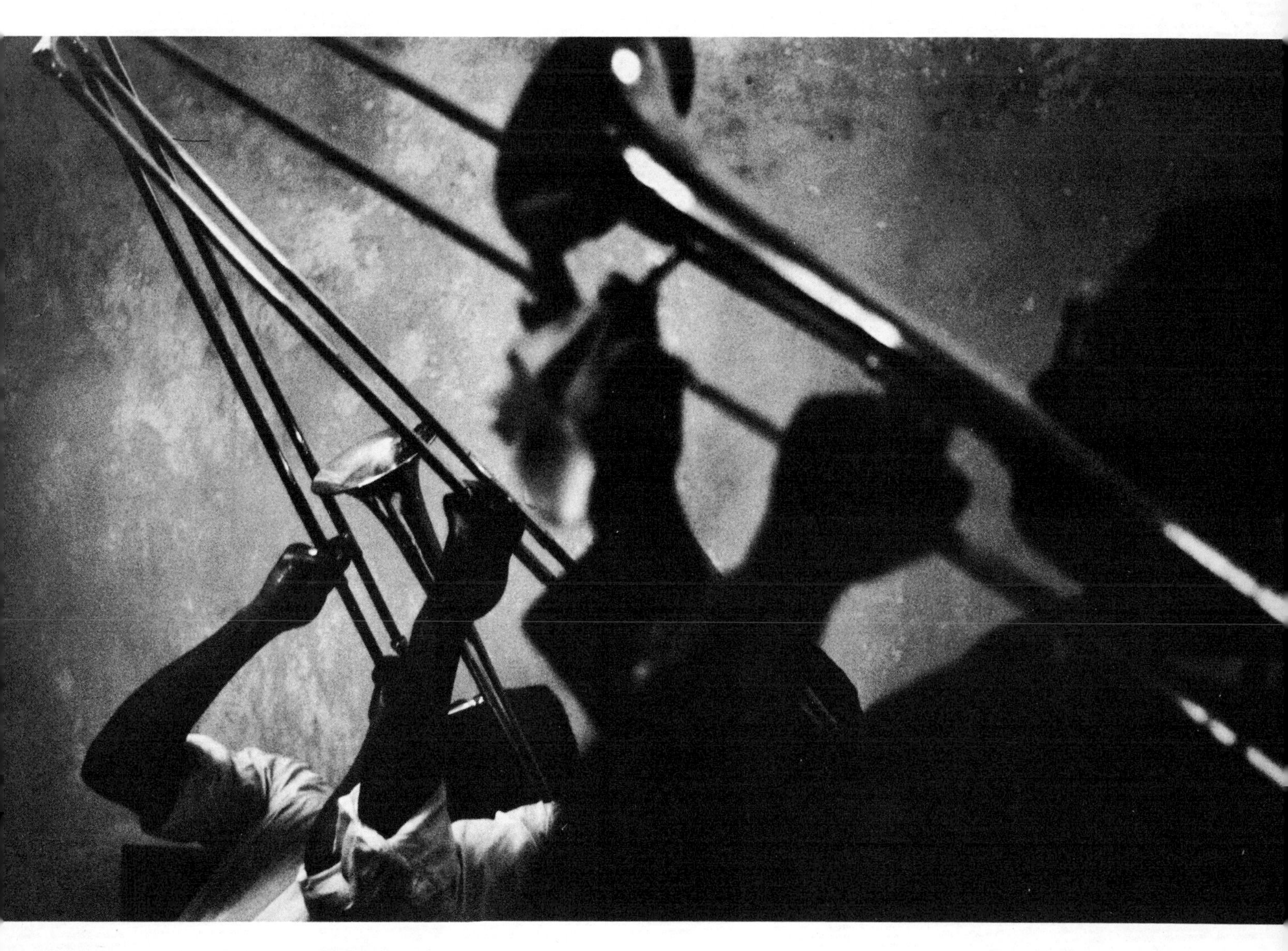

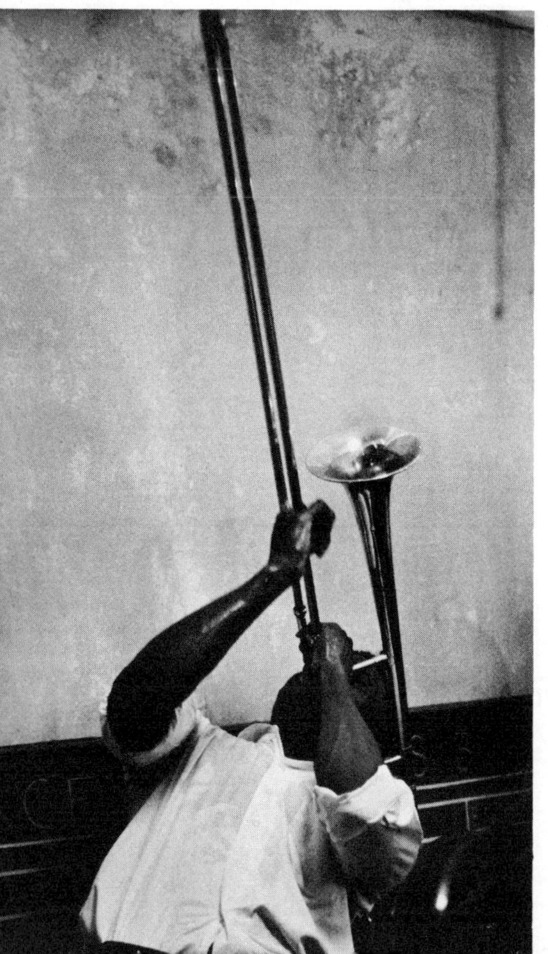

The United House of Prayer for All People of the Church on the Rock of the Apostolic Faith.

Above: Rabbi Matthew, leader of the Black Jews of Harlem, preaching in his synagogue.

Left: The late Malcolm X, before he broke away from the Black Muslim Movement.

ALLAH
IS THE
GREATEST

THE
YORUBA'S
OF
New Oyo (Harlem)
INVITE YOU TO A
BEME
A FESTIVAL AND BA
FOR THE GODS OF
AT AMERICA'S
YORU
TEM
28 WEST 116th ST.

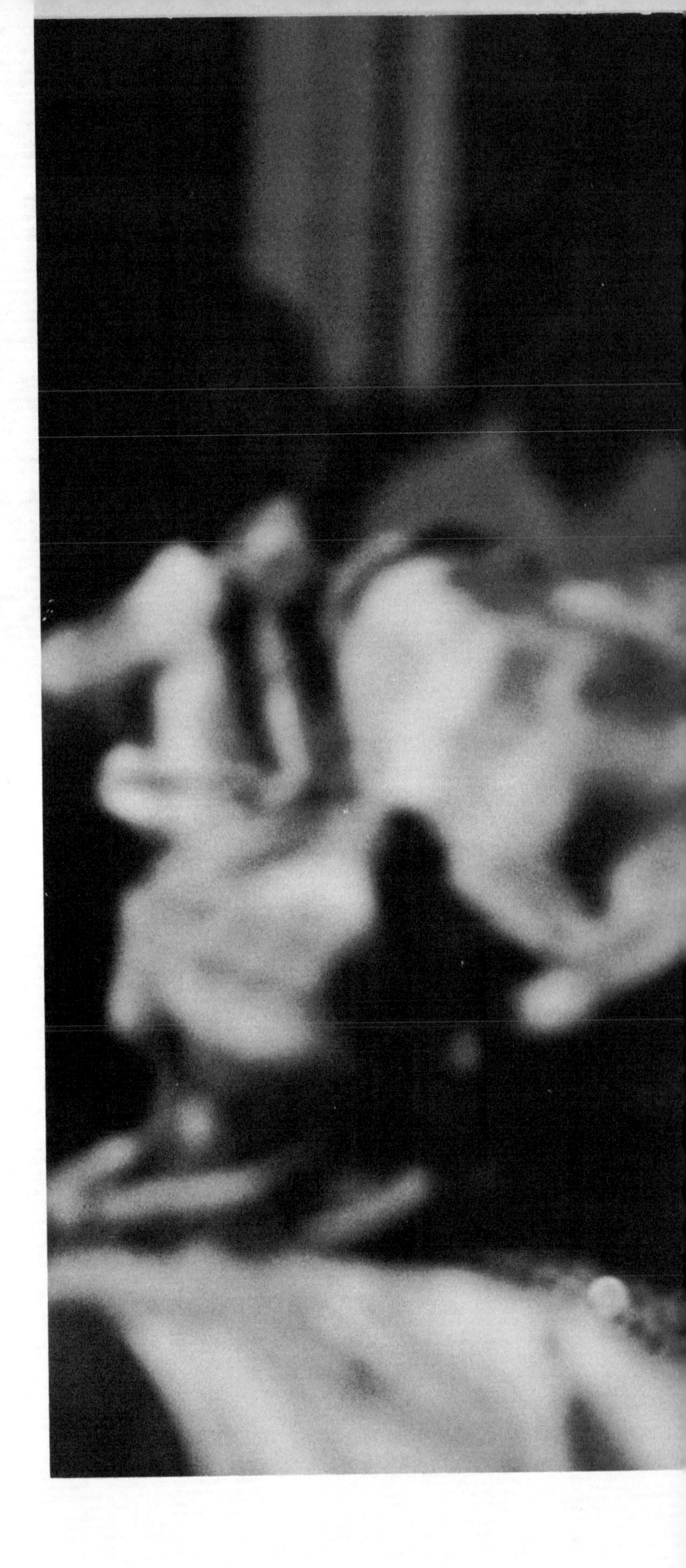

The Yoruba, whose temple on West 116th Street is incorporated as the African Theological Archministry, Inc.

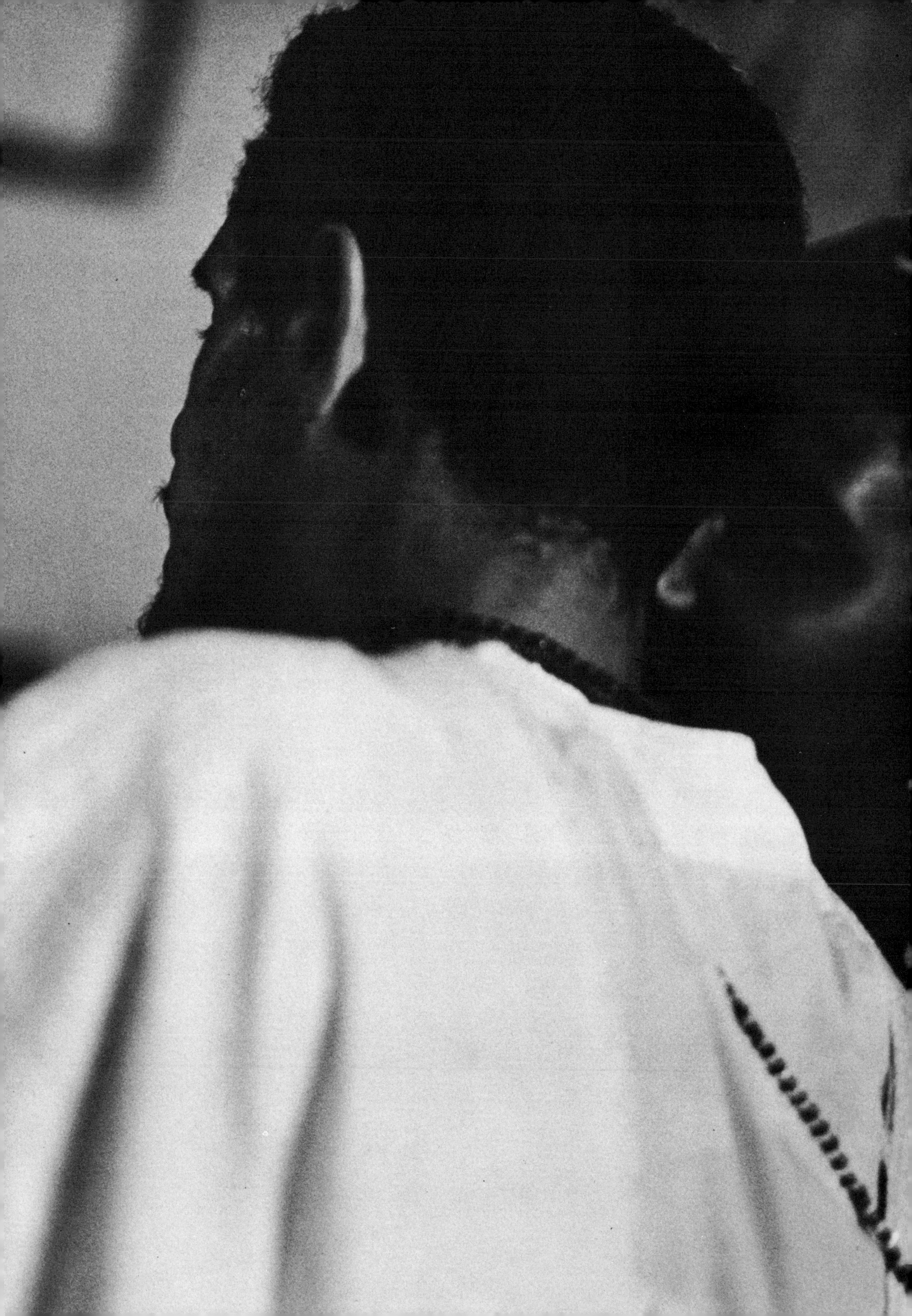

The American Buddhist Academy, Riverside Drive.

Below: Sen Soko, of Kyoto, performs the ancient tea ceremony at the American Buddhist Academy on Manhattan's Riverside Drive.

Upper right: Zen archery—a discipline which is at the same time a sport, an art and a ritual, in which accuracy is less vital than absolute perfection of form and control.

Lower right: These two men are members of one of the city's most exclusive athletic organizations, the Kendo Dojo or Kendo Club. Kendo is the ancient sport of the samurai, the Japanese warrior class, and its traditions go back unchanged to medieval times. The costumes worn by the two Kendo players for protection include samurai helmets, wood and cloth armor, black-lacquered breast plates and heavily padded blue skirts. Such protection is necessary: the weapon used is the *shinai*, a three-foot long, two-handed, bamboo sword that weighs two pounds. To avoid the blows of his opponent with this weapon (an imitation of the samurai sword), the player, who is barefooted, must be as agile as a dancer, yet powerful enough to counter with quick and heavy blows of his own.

Dr. R. Shibata, a master and instructor, says, "Kendo is more than good exercise: it is a hardening of all the senses." For here, too, the real purpose of the sport is self-discipline. Zen Buddhists, traditionally non-violent, believe that Kendo sublimates the aggressive tendencies and provides a field for that exactitude and precision which is central to Zen.

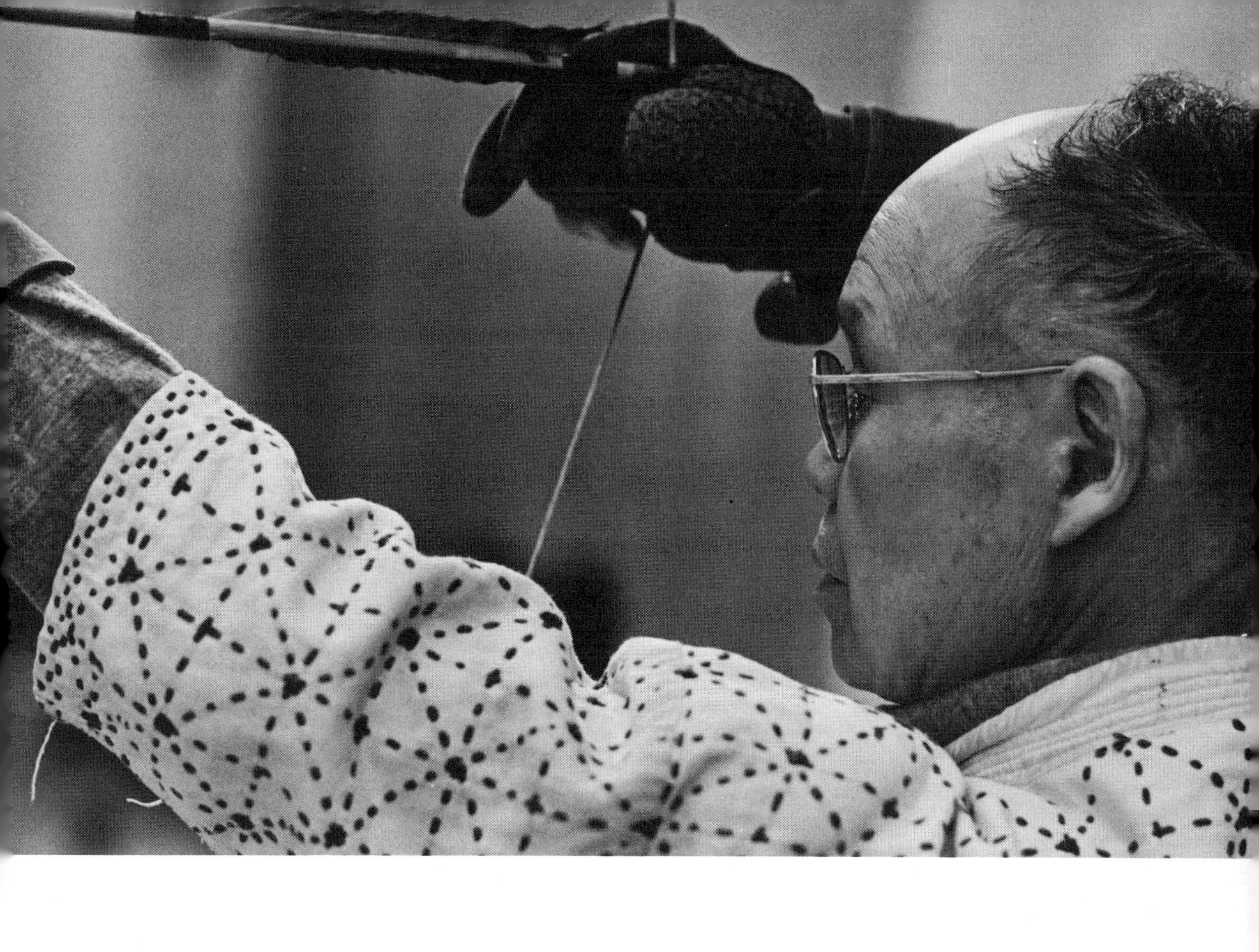

ISTALK
BAAL HATANY

Groundbreaking for a new Lubavicher Yeshiva, Brooklyn.

The festival of the Lag B'Omer—the ritual washing of the hands.

RIGHT: A Puerto Rican street evangelist.

The window of one of New York's one hundred *botanicas*, which sell, in the words of a recent investigator, "appurtenances of witchcraft and voodoo"—such as bat's blood at twenty-five cents an ounce, green candles guaranteed to bring money, yellow candles for gamblers, love charms, special perfumes to bring "peace at home," and, to rout one's enemies, "rattlesnake incense," a compound of "graveyard dust, dragons' blood and rattlesnake dung." Among other "charms" in this window are what appear to be a stuffed iguana, a crab and a shark fin. Incongruously enough, there are also Madonnas, holy statues and religious medals.

THE CHILDREN OF THE STREETS

NEW YORK is so glittering and dazzling, so constantly changing, one forgets that for children their street and their neighborhood is the world.

It is simple to look at a neighborhood and call it a slum. But a neighborhood is a neighborhood, even if it is run down and decaying, and those who grow up there do not spend all of their time agonizing over the conditions of their lives.

Can the city be cleansed of slums? Perhaps, but one doubts it. Can the slums be improved? Yes, certainly, and they must be. Yet the slums are not the subject of these photographs. Many of the children pictured here have grown up in what we call slums, some have not. But the important point is that they are *children* of New York, coming of age in the busy streets, learning to live in the shadow of the great buildings, to the rhythm of a busy city. Their faces often show it—a quickness, a fleeting glance of knowledge and experience older than their years, a sense of being trapped in a gigantic pattern of forces beyond their making or altering, of being absorbed into a life which has already been set for them. . . . But it may be our own pessimism and knowledge that reads this on their faces, for the wonder of New York is that children can grow up here as well as anywhere, that they make their own games and pleasures, that they survive by their own strength and individuality.

Out of the slums of the Lower East Side at the turn of the century came a generation of gifted men and women. Out of the slums of our own times will come another.

Even in the slums there is beauty for those children who have the eyes and the heart to see it. Here is how one teen-age boy, Delio Alfonso, described his street in Puerto Rican East Harlem, in a letter to a friend:

Well, Carol, let me describe some of the things that are going on in Harlem today. The sun is blazing like a flame on the top of wood, across the street from the Projects House there is the Park Avenue Banana Company and the doors are wide open and the sun is shining right into their store. Away from there is still

the old restaurant there, and the man all dressed up in a suit playing with the chain that holds the gate. And there is another man beside him with his fingers in his mouth. And there are people with children in carriages still going up and down the street to Park Avenue, little children running back and forth in the Candy Store trying to drive the man crazy for a candy bar. It's a great love down here today. It's like a flower garden in Harlem without a park, without a seed to plant. Ask me not how the flower grows but they grow without a root, but that is Harlem. You can hear the Mambo from the record shops, the rock and roll from the Candy Store, you can see the kids with the Pepsi-Cola, the Coke and the big fat man with a can of Ballantine or Rheingold. And pretty soon there will be people coming out with their checker boards and their dominoes playing on the side of the sidewalk, and soon the kids will be coming out with their drums. . . .

With love,
DELIO

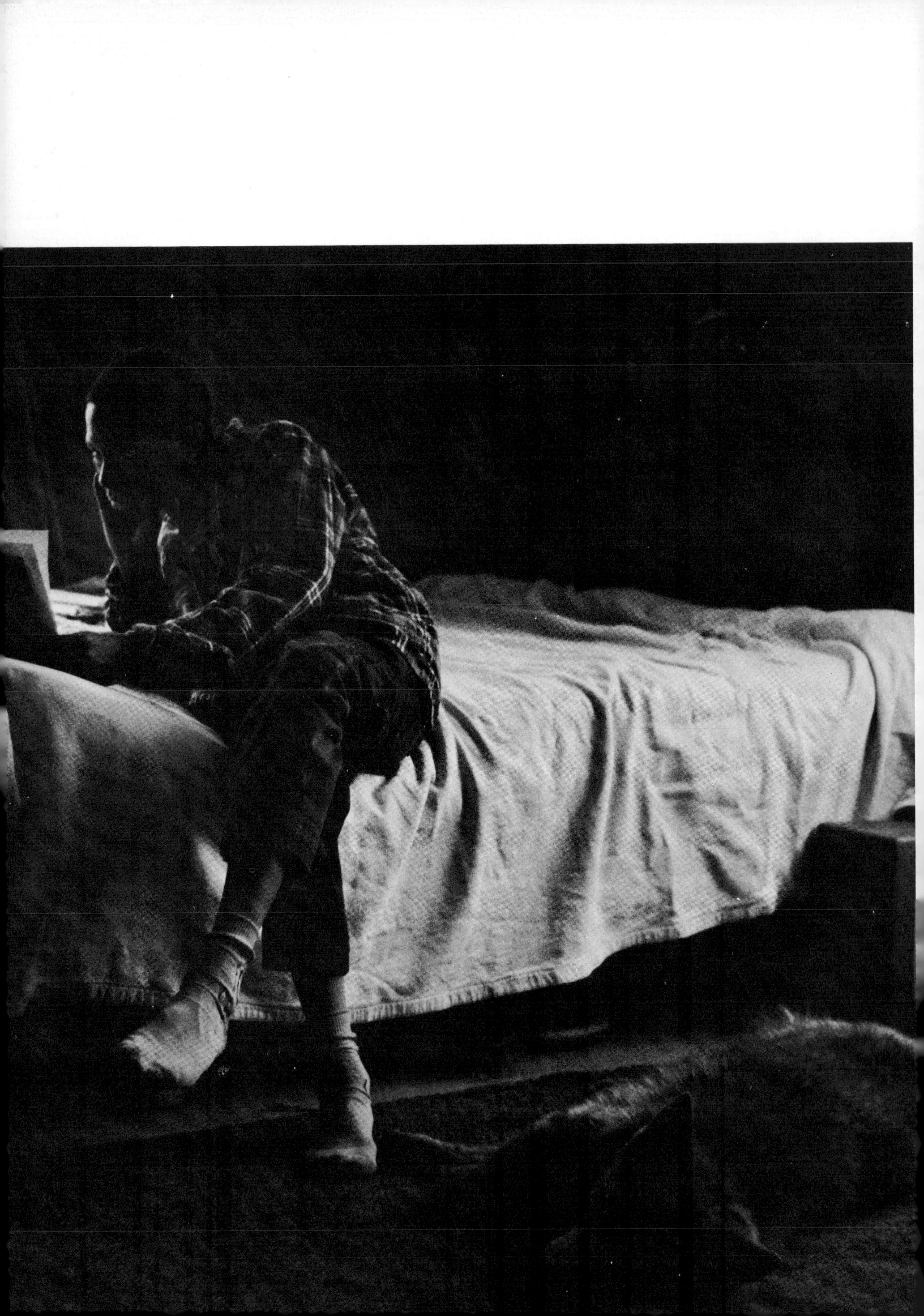

THE HELL WITH WORK!
SEX...
—ANYONE?
WORK FAST
TODAY YOU HAVE TO WORK LIKE A DOG
VICE PROBE
EXTRA
EVENING JOURNAL
VICE PROBE
CUFF LINK

KRASDALE
FANCY WHITE
SOLID PACK
TUNA
TENDER
PEAS
35

PATIO

IBANEZ

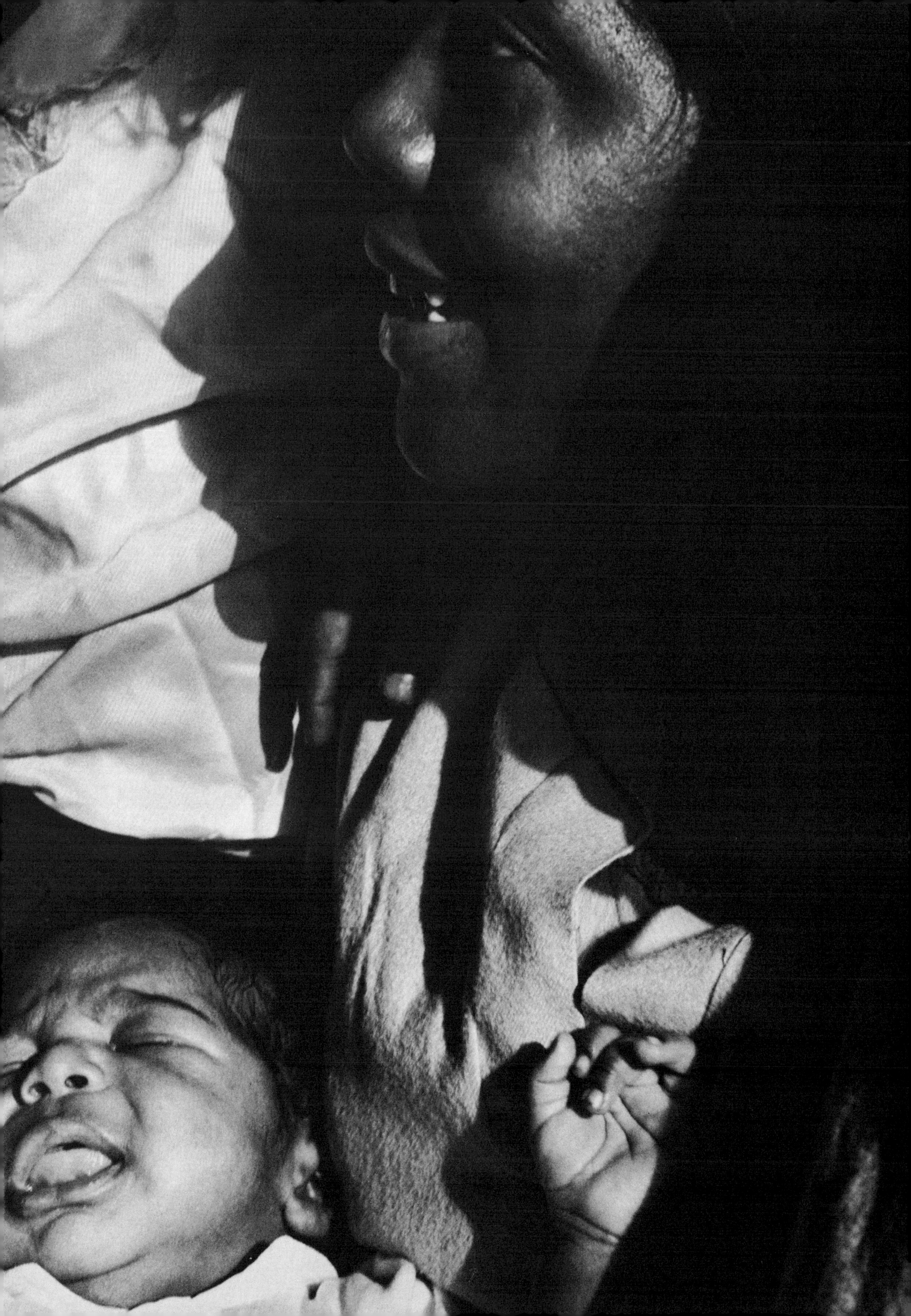

THE LONELY TOWN

Lonely house! Lonely me!
Funny with so many neighbors
How lonely it can be.
Oh, lonely street! Lonely town!
Funny you can be so lonely
With all these folks around.

—Lyrics by LANGSTON HUGHES
from *Street Scene* by Elmer
Rice and Kurt Weill

AGE AND POVERTY are the great vices of a big city—age, poverty and despair. If the city offers much, it demands much—youth, energy, hope and the potential of usefulness.

Many of the faces in this section are of those who seem alone, and those who have been abandoned. They are not faces to be pitied or sympathized with, they do not even demand indignation. They are simply a reflection of ourselves, alone as we sometimes are, alone as all of us someday will be. They are, quite simply, a part of the city, like the prosperous matrons sitting in the sun, waiting (but for what?) . . .

Their power to move has nothing to do with poverty, nor does this book.

They represent another world, a world apart. Like the Gypsies, the Hasidim, the Indians, the Black Jews, the Yoruba, we do not see them, or, if we do see them, we do not recognize them. New York, for so many, is a place where one comes to do something, a place in which one follows a career—but all around the office buildings and the apartment houses, there is a diversity of life that is a microcosm of the world, splintered, rich, varied, unfamiliar and sometimes agonizing. It is a world comparatively uninvolved in the familiar ambitions and folkways of modern America, a world in which there are few one-car families and no two-car families, a world which has little to do with Saturday night barbecues in the backyard, with the PTA, with com-

muting and mutual funds. It is not by any means the poorer for this. It is a world of older cultures, older traditions, of different ambitions and different realities. These people live in modern America, but are not *of* it. Some of them are anxious to become a part of it, but cannot; others, like the Hasidim, will go to great lengths to remain apart from it; still others, like the Indian steelworkers who top the high buildings, despise it, secure in a deep, ancestral knowledge of their own antiquity and uniqueness and worth.

The lonely are often dispossessed from that modern world too, sometimes because they want to be, sometimes because that world is intolerant of old age and unrealized ambitions.

PROGRAM MATERIALS
OPEN TO THE PUBLIC
BEWARE! WE HAVE NO MORE CHEEKS TO SPARE
WHY NOT IN ALABAMA?

44
Handi Pak
Kellogg's
1H24

THIS IS John Sergeant Cram, Jr., known for years to derelicts and drug addicts as "Mr. John." A member of one of New York's oldest and most aristocratic families, his great-great-grandfather was the beloved Peter Cooper, the inventor and industrialist who gave Cooper Union to the city. His great-grandfather was Edward Cooper, who was New York's mayor eighty-five years ago. His father was a distinguished lawyer. His mother was a reformer, who fought for woman's suffrage, worked to end the exploitation of underpaid clothing workers and was a pacifist through both World Wars.

Mr. Cram studied at Princeton and Oxford, served for three years as a librarian and a clerk with the Armed Forces during World War II, but never had a job as a civilian until he was past forty-five. A quiet-spoken, gentle bachelor with a futile air, Mr. Cram was appalled to learn one day that there were derelicts in the city, most of them unemployed foreign seamen, who were ineligible for relief, and whom no charitable organization was interested in helping. Many of them could not speak English, and there were many alcoholics and drug addicts among them.

Cram decided that someone had to do something for these lost men who had been abandoned by society, to give them at least food enough to keep alive and a place to sleep. At first he used buildings owned by his mother. But these were sold after she died in 1960. For two hundred dollars a month Cram rented a dusty loft on Fifth Avenue and 104th Street that had been used as a dance hall long ago. It was two hundred feet long, and, in memory of happier days, a few dusty colored paper balls dangled from the ceiling. At one end there was a little platform on which the band had once played. Mr. Cram sat on this in his rocking chair, a table at his side for the sandwiches and bottles of Coca-Cola he served his guests. For those who had no other place to sleep there were mattresses on the floor.

He had been there seven months on the night in 1961 when the police raided the place. They found among the thirty derelicts six narcotics suspects, whom they arrested. On finding two hypodermic needles they also arrested Mr. Cram, who admitted they were his. They charged him also with "harboring narcotics users."

The headline in the New York *Daily News* next day read:

RICH BEATNIK: IT'S NOT ODD TO SQUARE WITH DERELICTS

When the magistrate who heard the case learned that Mr. Cram used the hypodermic needles to give himself injections for the relief of a deficiency in his adrenal glands, he released him. Cram went back to the loft building. He told reporters he did not know that some of his guests were addicts. Helping them cost him about one thousand dollars a month. He intended to continue helping them. "My door was always open," he said. "They came in even when I was asleep. If you give them a dollar or a million dollars they drink it all up. But they do need food and a little help once in a while. . . . I don't know that it does any good. But it does no harm."

BELOW: A Puerto Rican beggar, with the staff and crucifix of a Spanish pilgrim.

Since 1891
SINCE 1891
KERN
HAM
BACON
SAUSAGE
COLD CUTS
FRANKFURTS
SPECIALTIES
GEO. KERN
350 W. 38 ST.

Lichee
荔枝
CHEE
HEE

Spanish East Harlem—the faces of the young.

"BIG
BOSCO
BEAR"
TONY

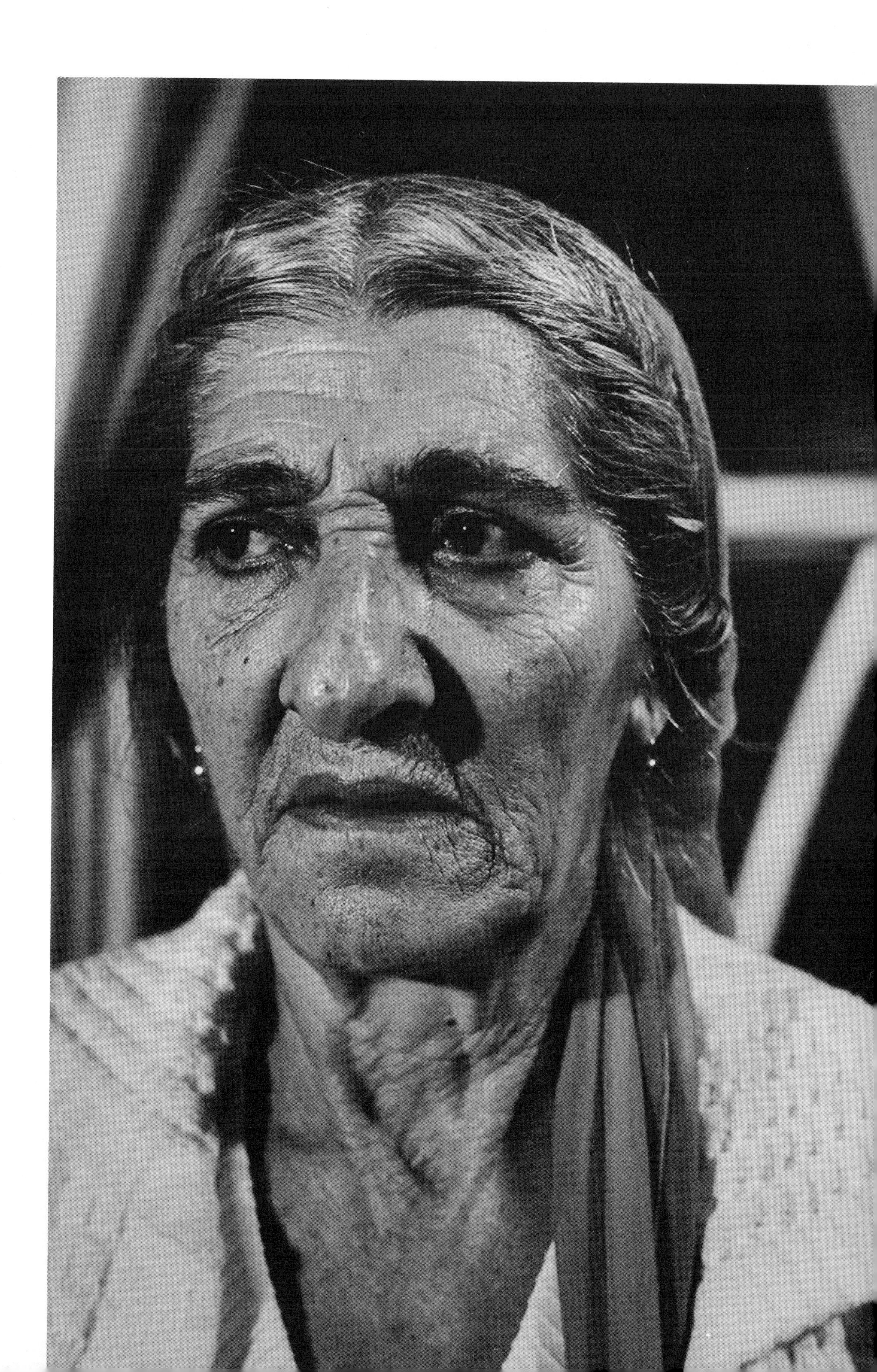

LIVE JAZZ
THE
WALL STR
JOURNA
THE TWIST
25¢

THE HAPPIEST DAY

NEW YORK'S WEDDINGS reflect in romantic terms the variety and international flavor and color of her daily life.

Each year New Yorkers are united in wedding ceremonies performed in almost every language spoken on earth, including Flemish, Hindustani, Chinese, Japanese, Greek, Russian, Arabic and Swahili. Each day scores of couples are married in New York's bridal chapel in the Municipal Building by the City Clerk whose fee is three dollars, including the certificate. For special occasions, the Mayor himself takes time out of his busy life to marry people, and so do hundreds of city judges.

Wealthy families still spend fortunes for wedding receptions in the city's great hotels, often following a ceremony in a fashionable Fifth Avenue church. The weddings of the Astors, Goulds and Vanderbilts were always front-page news in the days when the world was a more light-hearted place. In the sixties one has to seek on the society page the details of what the bride wore, the list of her attendants and the groom's, and the important guests. In fact, the city's aristocrats seem to have lost their interest in magnificent weddings, and the traditional elegances are, strangely, best observed in the part of town where one would least expect to find them—Harlem. Where else can one still see the men, young and old, in morning coats and striped trousers, sometimes carrying a cane?

The wedding of Hasidic Jews is, unlike so many of their functions and holidays, performed in a somewhat solemn spirit, and always outdoors, under a canopy called the "*Chuppah.*" The bride is led to this by her father, the groom by his mother. As in other orthodox weddings, the couple drink from a goblet of wine during the ceremony. The glass is then crushed underfoot by the bridegroom. After this has been done, the festivities begin, with joy and delight—for does not God wish to be worshipped in a happy spirit?

No less joyful, but far less identified with a religious tradition, are the marriage ceremonies of Gypsies. Though most New Yorkers are unaware of it, the city is one of the most important meeting grounds in the endless and worldwide migrations of Gypsies. Other peoples emigrate from their homelands to *stay* in another country, but the Gypsies *travel,* back and forth in ceaseless movement, very often using the airplane, the boat and the train as they once used the caravan. Indeed, they move, at will, from one world to another. A Gypsy family may be in New York one year, fortunetelling; the next year in South America, repairing pots and pans; another year, and they may be in the Balkans, traveling in the traditional caravan over the long, slow, dusty roads. For, almost by definition, the Gypsies know no frontiers, recognize no barriers, use every means to increase their range of travel, adopt any language or custom that seems expected of them . . . all the while retaining their individual culture, their language—Romany—their distinctive dress, their overwhelming sense of identity with themselves and their separation from the *gajo*, the outsider.

The Gypsy wedding is a part of this identity, a part of their custom and their traditions. Indeed, it is symbolic of their whole outlook on life—a blend of shrewdness and heroic enjoyment.

The basic principle of the Gypsy wedding is purely practical: the acquisition of the bride, who is usually, but not always, more than thirteen years old, and who must be a virgin. She must be purchased by the groom's father, and the dowry payment is anywhere between two thousand and ten thousand dollars, payable exclusively in gold coins. (The wealth of a Gypsy family is always carried in gold coins. On festive occasions, the women often wear them around their necks, like immensely heavy necklaces, badges of status and wealth in the community.)

Romance plays little or no part in Gypsy weddings—they believe that true love will grow out of sharing a common life, and that the Western conception of romantic love is painful and temporary. Instead, the marriage is based on family alliances and the interests of the tribe. For this reason, the wedding is not centered on the bride and groom—they are pawns of no particular importance, and, being young, they must in any case defer to their elders. Instead, the wedding is a gathering, an occasion to meet old friends, to gossip, sing, drink, dance and eat. Lavish hospitality is taken for granted

—the Gypsy is naturally lavish—and the food and the drink go on for days and days. The wedding ceremony itself is simple—the bride and the groom share bread and salt—and hurried. The main thing is the celebration, in all its Gargantuan enjoyment.

In these photographs, the wedding is taking place in the Polski Dom Narodowy, in St. Mark's Place, but the spirit, the flash of the gold coins, the bride's dress, the family elders, all are a part of a tradition that is infinitely old and almost completely concealed from the casual outsider. Like the Gypsies singing their sad and guttural songs in the pictures on pages 112–113, they are a world apart, visitors to New York, not settlers, living in the city briefly, never becoming a part of it. Most of the time they are invisible: sometimes a wedding or a fortunetelling parlor brings them to our attention. Yet, in a curious way, they are an essential part of the life of a great city like New York—for there has never been a great cosmopolitan city without Gypsies, and, in all likelihood, there never will be.

TOWAWAY ZONE

A Gypsy wedding, in the Polski Dom Narodowy, St. Mark's Place. The bride, left, wears, as a mark of honor, her new family's wealth of gold pieces, smaller now by the amount it cost her father-in-law to purchase her.

THE SEVENTH DAY

It is the city of the Good Time, and the Good Time is there so sacred that you may be excused anything you do in searching for it.
FORD MADOX FORD

Like the art of conversation, self-entertainment is said to be disappearing from American life. But not in New York.

CHINATOWN'S MEN, women and children in their self-made amusements pay homage both to the remote past and to today. Their professional theater on the Bowery disappeared years ago with the rest of the landmarks on that strange old street. But the amateurs and semi-professional troupes still carry on in school auditoriums, the Chinese community center and wherever else they can. Nothing is changed in these performances.

Today, as for centuries past, they wear the same costumes, speak the same lines in the old shows that date back almost to the days of antiquity. The costumes are kept in teakwood chests between performances and are worn by succeeding generations until they fall apart. Then new ones precisely like them are made by the loving hands of experts without a detail being changed or different stitching in the silk or satin robes.

The Chinese drum-majorette on page 105 is in startling contrast to the glittering, traditional panoply of the Chinese opera; she is a symbol of the way in which tradition and the life of modern America become inextricably

mixed. Her school is entirely Chinese: it teaches in Chinese exclusively; the marching band is one of the very few American intrusions permitted in this Chinese world, where the curriculum, the language, the discipline and the spirit remain, in every other way, entirely that of China. It is the result of a very wise decision on the part of the Chinese community to retain, so far as possible, their own culture and traditions within the framework of a different world.

More American, more reminiscent of a less stylized past, is the motorcycle club, some of whose members are shown here. "The Wild Ones"? Perhaps in appearance, but not in reality—for this group of motorcyclists consists largely of married men, who roar off not to terrorize small towns (though there is something inescapably terrifying about any large group of motorcyclists), but to peaceful picnics in New Jersey. It may seem remarkable that this is a Negro motorcycle club. But why? The integration of schools may be a difficult process, but despite whatever else separates us from our fellow Americans, our pleasures are the same: perhaps this is the only truly common culture we have.

There is no end to the joys and pleasures of New York, nor to their diversities and peculiarities. On the West Side, pigeon-fanciers race their birds—there are even bookmakers who specialize in this somewhat esoteric sport. Folk singers (triumphant after a battle with the city's laws) gather, in the summer, in Washington Square. For visitors, New York may be—is—a town of garish pleasures, but that is a different New York. The images here are of people who take their pleasures in the environment of the city, pleasures that perhaps only a great city can provide.

CHINESE PUBLIC SCHOOL
N.Y.C.

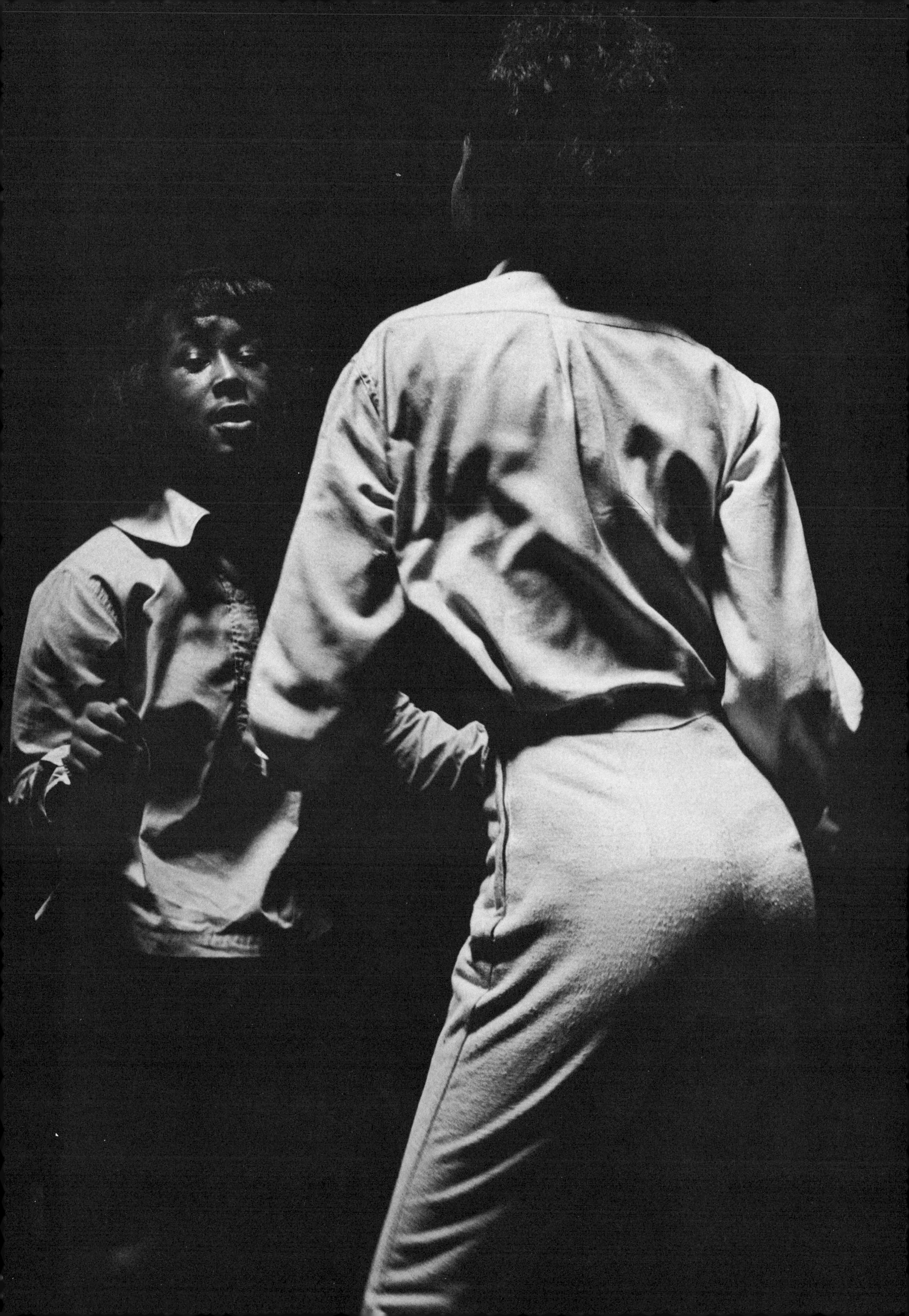

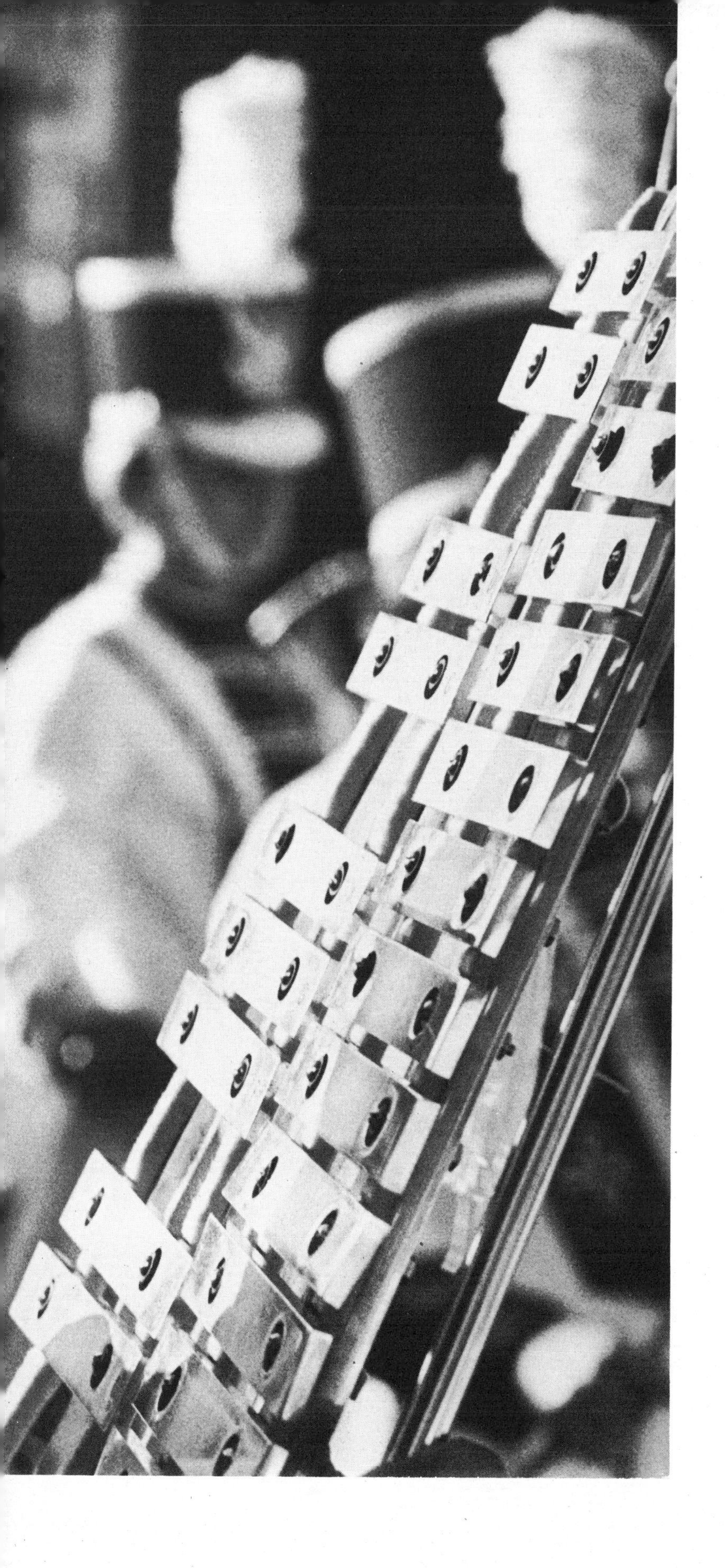

ED199
NJ
63

LOEW'S
MANIAC WITH A MACHINE GUN
"MAD DOG COLL"
VICE AND VIOLENCE
"UNDERWORLD U S A"

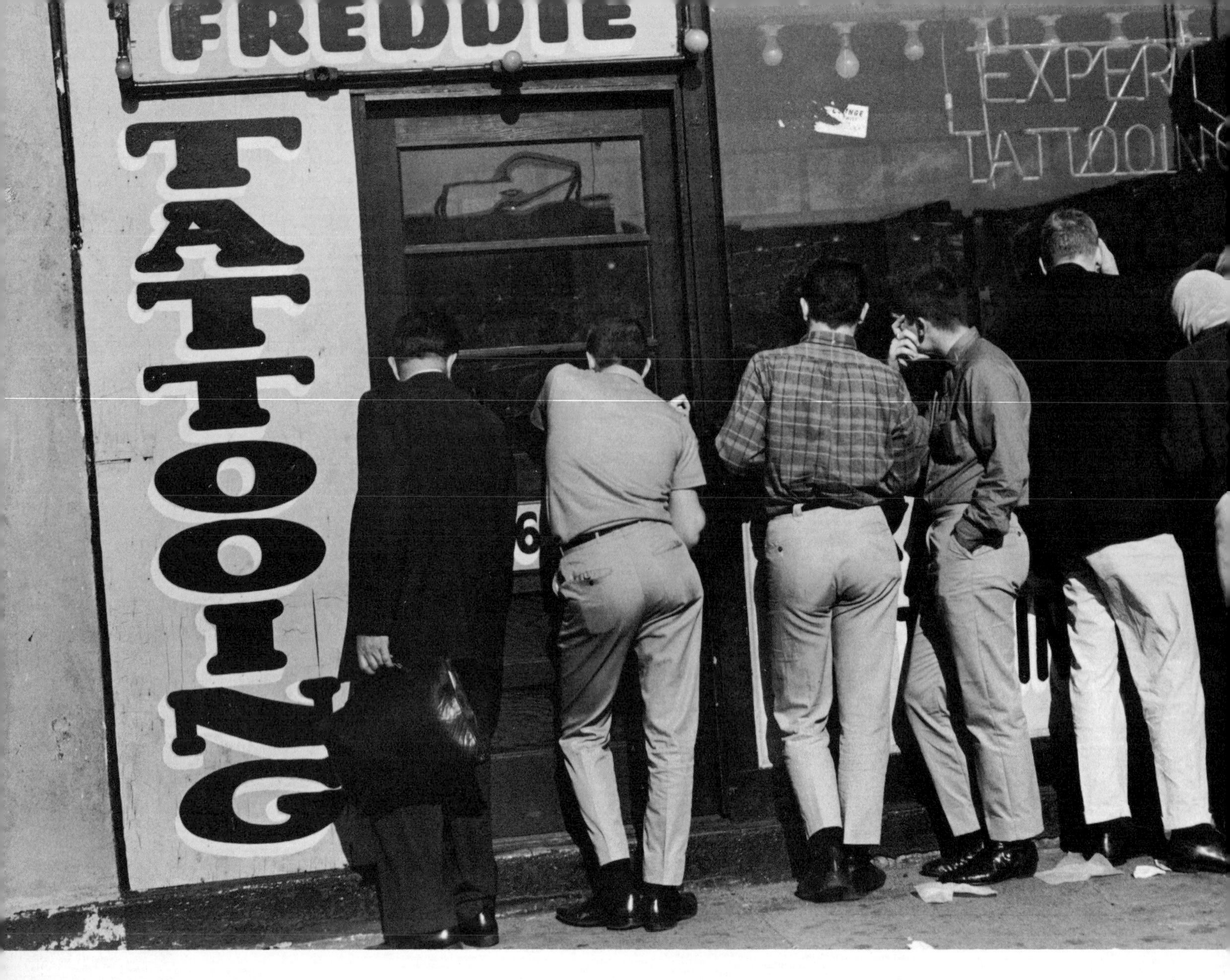

Summer: Coney Island.

Summer: East Harlem.

CHANGE AND DECAY

IN ONE YEAR alone $900,000,000 was spent to tear down 8,095 New York buildings and complete the construction of 12,000 new ones. Perhaps most of the buildings were rightfully destroyed. They were rotting, blackening eyesores or had merely outlived their usefulness.

But no structure was spared for its beauty or its past. New York is not one of the small number of American communities with laws against destruction of beautiful buildings and landmarks. If someone can make money by destroying and rebuilding and has the necessary financing, there is little to stop him. Even the slim, graceful skyscrapers are not immune to this sort of massive vandalism in the interest of money-making.

Many famous old New York streets—even whole neighborhoods—have already disappeared. In the housing developments or clusters of business buildings that replaced them there is nothing linking that part of the city with its past. Old residents, coming back, search in vain for much trace of the life they lived, the friends and neighbors they knew and played cards with or argued with about politics and religion and the mysterious whims of their women.

Despite the trend toward comformity, the incongruities and startling contrasts of New York remain.

A boy's kite sails triumphantly over the tin and tar roofs patched up by an amateur repairman, over the smog and the smoke into the clear blue sky above, carrying the dreams of its twelve-year-old owner high above it. For the great steaming city of legend is, in fact, an ever-changing patchwork quilt of old and new, half shiny steel, half an improvisation of tar and tin.

On the rooftops of Spanish Harlem—"El Barrio"—Puerto Rican children have revived the old game of kite-flying as a kind of aerial battle. A razor blade is tied to the string of the kite. On seeing another kite go up, the first boy tries to maneuver his kite above and beyond it. The trick then is to drop his line over that of the other boy and draw it in so that he cuts the line. The rule of the game is that the fallen kite belongs to the razor-blade wielder—if he can recover it.

The last photographs in this book—particularly the very last one—are evocative—though they will hardly seem to be at first sight—of a great people and a great legend. They are Indians—the Mohawks and other Iroquois whose specialty is rigging the beams and structures of skyscrapers and bridges. They work only on the highest level—theirs is a job that calls for sure footwork, instinctive courage and a fierce, even contemptuous pride.

They call themselves "connectors" or "pushers," and they earn, at times, as much as two thousand dollars a month. When they are working, they live together on Atlantic Avenue, in Brooklyn; when they are between jobs, or on weekends, they return to their reservations in Caughnawaga, in Canada. (The reservation itself is curious and unique, for it was founded in 1667 by Louis XIV, as a Catholic mission to the Indians, and still possesses a silver chalice presented by the Sun King. Until the recent Ecumenical decision, the Mohawks were the only people with the privilege of using their vernacular at all liturgical functions, including High Mass, and one may still hear today, as in centuries past, Palestrina's "Adoramus te, Christe" sung in Indian dialect.)

Their names are given to them at birth by the midwife, and based on the first thing that strikes her eyes—Summer Sky, Deep Snow, Little Star, Scattered Pines, etc.—but each Indian also has a Christian name which he uses outside the reservation. Traditionalists in every respect, the Indians on Atlantic Avenue still believe in what they call "The Long Hope"—when the Americas will revert to the Indians. . . .

In the meantime, they work in the white man's world and, secure in their invisible steel heights, they observe the life around them during their breaks, using a telescope, like the Indian spies and scouts of an earlier and more heroic age.

ITT

BETHLEHEM

Ng Ka Py
Liqueur
"Orange Peel Flavored"
9.95
香港
五加皮
永利威
HONG KONG
1.70
5.40